Radiant Ruth the Rhino Shines Bright

by AJ Sarcione

The sun peeks through the trees as Radiant Ruth the Rhino wakes up smiling. She's ready for another adventurous day. Yawning, she says:

I spark a spark, I shine.
I think with both
my heart and mind.

Radiant Ruth takes her morning bath and sees a day full of possibilities. Maybe today she will find the pot of gold at the end of the rainbow. Or discover a new plant to eat. Or make a new friend. She says:

I spark a spark, I shine.
If I can dream it, it's
only a matter of time.

Radiant Ruth runs to meet eight of her friends for breakfast. She finds a new plant along the way. Excited to stop and eat it, she knows her friends are waiting for her. She says:

I spark a spark, I shine.
I'll bring this as a gift
and cut it up in nine.

Radiant Ruth arrives with the plant cut up for her and her friends. But wait, there's someone new. Now there's ten in total instead of nine. Does that mean the new friend doesn't get any? she says:

2

10

9

1

3

4

5

6

7

8

I spark a spark, I shine.
I can find another new plant.
Here, you can have mine.

They all go to find more food and come across some mud. Radiant Ruth doesn't like playing in the mud. She tries to get her friends to run instead. But everyone jumps in. So she says:

I spark a spark, I shine.
We don't all have to like the same things, it's fine. And if my idea isn't chosen, I don't whine.

A cloud passes by and it starts to rain. With the sun still shining, Radiant Ruth and her friends look and what do they see? A rainbow! They run to find the pot of gold. As they get closer, the rainbow starts to disappear. Oh no! But Radiant Ruth says:

I spark a spark, I shine.
Look around. All that's here is me
and all of you, and it's a sign. The
pot of gold is all of you nine.

The end of the day nears and Radiant Ruth and her friends head back towards home. After finding a new plant, a new friend, and the end of the rainbow, Radiant Ruth gets ready to sleep and says:

What I believed came true, and putting others feelings first brought me someone new. We found the pot of gold, and it was more perfect than I was told. Every day I'll continue to say, I think with both my heart and mind.

I spark a spark, I shine.

The End

CPSIA information can be obtained
at www.ICGtesting.com
Printed in the USA
BVHW020500251120
594076BV00002B/11